Let's Discover Canada

NOVA SCOTIA

by
Suzanne LeVert

George Sheppard
McMaster University
General Editor

CHELSEA HOUSE PUBLISHERS

New York   Philadelphia

Cover: Lunenburg, Nova Scotia.
Opposite: The province's Scottish heritage is celebrated by bagpipers in the coastal town of Antigonish.

Chelsea House Publishers
EDITOR-IN-CHIEF: Remmel Nunn
MANAGING EDITOR: Karyn Gullen Browne
COPY CHIEF: Mark Rifkin
PICTURE EDITOR: Adrian G. Allen
ART DIRECTOR: Maria Epes
ASSISTANT ART DIRECTOR: Noreen Romano
MANUFACTURING DIRECTOR: Gerald Levine
SYSTEMS MANAGER: Lindsey Ottman
PRODUCTION MANAGER: Joseph Romano
PRODUCTION COORDINATOR: Marie Claire Cebrián

Let's Discover Canada
SENIOR EDITOR: Rebecca Stefoff

Staff for NOVA SCOTIA
COPY EDITOR: Benson D. Simmonds
EDITORIAL ASSISTANT: Ian Wilker
PICTURE RESEARCHER: Patricia Burns
DESIGNER: Diana Blume

Copyright © 1992 by Chelsea House Publishers, a division of Main Line Book Co. All rights reserved. Printed and bound in the United States of America.

First Printing

1   3   5   7   9   8   6   4   2

Library of Congress Cataloging-in-Publication Data

LeVert, Suzanne.
    Let's discover Canada. Nova Scotia/by Suzanne LeVert; George Sheppard, general editor.
        p.   cm.
    Includes bibliographical references and index.
    Summary: Discusses the geography, history, and culture of the Canadian province
of Nova Scotia.
    ISBN 0-7910-1028-7
    1. Nova Scotia—Juvenile literature.   [1. Nova Scotia.]
    I. Sheppard, George C. B. II. Title   91-20786
    F1037.4.L48   1992   CIP
    971.6—dc20   AC

Contents

My Canada

by Pierre Berton

"Nobody knows my country," a great Canadian journalist, Bruce Hutchison, wrote almost half a century ago. It is still true. Most Americans, I think, see Canada as a pleasant vacationland and not much more. And yet we are the United States's greatest single commercial customer, and the United States is our largest customer.

Lacking a major movie industry, we have made no widescreen epics to chronicle our triumphs and our tragedies. But then there has been little blood in our colonial past—no revolutions, no civil war, not even a wild west. Yet our history is crammed with remarkable men and women. I am thinking of Joshua Slocum, the first man to sail alone around the world, and Robert Henderson, the prospector who helped start the Klondike gold rush. I am thinking of some of our famous artists and writers—comedian Dan Aykroyd, novelists Margaret Atwood and Robertson Davies, such popular performers as Michael J. Fox, Anne Murray, Gordon Lightfoot, and k.d. lang, and hockey greats from Maurice Richard to Gordie Howe to Wayne Gretzky.

The real shape of Canada explains why our greatest epic has been the building of the Pacific Railway to unite the nation from

sea to sea in 1885. On the map, the country looks square. But because the overwhelming majority of Canadians live within 100 miles (160 kilometers) of the U.S. border, in practical terms the nation is long and skinny. We are in fact an archipelago of population islands separated by implacable barriers—the angry ocean, three mountain walls, and the Canadian Shield, that vast desert of billion-year-old rock that sprawls over half the country, rich in mineral treasures, impossible for agriculture.

Canada's geography makes the country difficult to govern and explains our obsession with transportation and communication. The government has to be as involved in railways, airlines, and broadcasting networks as it is with social services such as universal medical care. Rugged individualism is not a Canadian quality. Given the environment, people long ago learned to work together for security.

It is ironic that the very bulwarks that separate us—the chiseled peaks of the Selkirk Mountains, the gnarled scarps north of Lake Superior, the ice-choked waters of the Northumberland Strait —should also be among our greatest attractions for tourists and artists. But if that is the paradox of Canada, it is also the glory.

Wrapped in mist, Peggy's Cove is one of many small fishing villages scattered about the inlets and bays of Nova Scotia's long seacoast.

CANADA

UNITED STATES

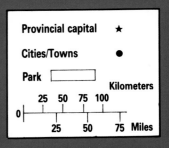

Provincial capital ★

Cities/Towns ●

Park ▭

Kilometers

0   25   50   75 100

25   50   75   Miles

GULF OF ST. LAWRENCE

CABOT STRAIT

North Barren

Cheticamp

Cape Breton Highlands Nat'l Pk.

PRINCE EDWARD ISLAND

L. Bras d'Or

Sydney

Glace Bay

NEW BRUNSWICK

NORTHUMBERLAND STRAIT

Louisbourg

Isthmus of Chignecto

CHIGNECTO BAY

Springhill

New Glasgow

COBEQUID MTNS.

St. Mary's R.

Antigonish

STRAIT OF CANSO

MINAS BASIN

Truro

MAINE

BAY OF FUNDY

Shubenacadie R.

Annapolis R.

Wolfville

New Germany

ATLANTIC

Annapolis Royal

Dartmouth

ST. MARY'S BAY

Meteghan

Halifax

OCEAN

Kejimkujik Nat'l Pk.

Lunenburg

Yarmouth

Shelburne

Mersey R.

Sable Island

L. Rossignol

NOVA SCOTIA

Mayflower

Nova Scotia at a Glance

Population: 873,199 (1986 census); 7th among provinces in population

Area: 21,423 square miles (55,490 square kilometers); 9th among provinces in area

Capital: Halifax (population 113,577)

Other cities: Dartmouth (65,243), Sydney (27,754), Glace Bay (20,467)

Entered Dominion of Canada: July 1, 1867

Principal products: Milk, pork products, lobsters, paper products, coal, gypsum

Motto: *Munit Haec at Altera Vincit* (One defends and the other conquers)

Provincial flower: Trailing arbutus, also called mayflower

Provincial coat of arms: The cross of St. Andrew and the arms of Scotland, with a Native Canadian representing the province's original inhabitants and a royal unicorn representing England; adopted in 1626

Provincial flag: The cross of St. Andrew and the coat of arms of Scotland; adopted in 1626

Government: A parliamentary system with a legislature of 52 members who are elected by district for terms of 5 years; the formal head of state is the lieutenant governor, who is appointed by the federal government as a representative of the British crown; the head of government is the premier, who is the leader of the party in power; the premier appoints an executive council from the legislature; Nova Scotia is represented in the federal government in Ottawa by 10 senators and 11 members of the House of Commons

The Land

The province of Nova Scotia is almost completely surrounded by water and has often been referred to as the Wharf of North America and as Canada's Ocean Playground. Jutting out into the Atlantic Ocean, the province is shaped a bit like a giant lobster snatching with spread claws at the neighboring province of Newfoundland. Nova Scotia is connected to the province of New Brunswick and the rest of Canada by a 17-mile-wide (27-kilometer-wide) strip of land called the Isthmus of Chignecto. No spot in Nova Scotia is more than 35 miles (56 kilometers) from the sea.

The province's location has shaped its overall development. Nova Scotia is a significant strategic site, overlooking the sea approach to North America from Europe. Halifax, the capital, has become both an important shipping port and one of the continent's key portals for European immigrants. The location has economic importance, too: The waters around the province are among the most productive and valuable fishing grounds in the world.

Opposite: Basalt cliffs tower above the sea on Brier Island off the Nova Scotia shore. Most of the 3,800 or so offshore islands are uninhabited; hikers and bird-watchers occasionally visit them.
Above: Winter at Ingonish, near the northern tip of Cape Breton Island.

Nova Scotia is one of the four Atlantic Provinces of Canada; the others are New Brunswick, Newfoundland, and Prince Edward Island. (Nova Scotia, New Brunswick, and Prince Edward Island are also called the Maritime Provinces.) North of Nova Scotia are the Northumberland Strait, the Gulf of St. Lawrence, and the Cabot Strait. On the east, south, and southwest lies the Atlantic Ocean. On the west and northwest are the Bay of Fundy and the province of New Brunswick.

Nova Scotia has two parts, the mainland peninsula and an island called Cape Breton. The mainland and the island are separated by a channel called the Strait of Canso, which is only .75 miles (1.2 kilometers) wide at its narrowest point; it is bridged by a causeway. About 3,800 small islands, most of them uninhabited, lie off the province's coast. The largest of these is Sable Island, a 25-mile-long (38-kilometer-long) sandbar situated about 170 miles (300 kilometers) east of Halifax. Before lighthouses were installed, many ships crashed against the ever-shifting sandy shores of Sable Island. There were so many wrecks that the island was called the Graveyard of the Atlantic. Today Sable Island is best known for the large deposits of oil and natural gas that lie under the seabed off its shores.

Nova Scotia's most striking physical feature is its coastline. Wrapping around the many islands and surrounding nearly all of the mainland, the coastline is about 4,700 miles (7,579 kilometers) long—an astounding distance for a province that is Canada's second smallest (after Prince Edward Island). Nova Scotia's coastline is long in relation to the province's size because the coastline is quite irregular, deeply indented with bays and fjords and punctuated with many promontories and peninsulas.

Nova Scotia's 21,423 square miles (55,490 square kilometers) contain a varied and scenic topography. The province has low but rugged mountain highlands, gentle valleys, and numerous lakes, rivers, and streams. It also has scores of picturesque villages and towns, as well as the cities of Halifax, Dartmouth, and Sydney.

Nova Scotia consists of two main types of terrain, the Atlantic upland and the coastal lowlands. The upland is a series

The Margaree Valley in western Cape Breton. Good agricultural land is scarce in Nova Scotia; farms and pastures tend to be concentrated along the lowland rivers.

of hilly ranges covered with thick pine and birch forests. These ranges run through the center of the province, extending from the southwestern part of the mainland to northeastern Cape Breton Island. In the central part of the peninsula, near the Isthmus of Chignecto, this upland ridge is called the Cobequid Mountains. On Cape Breton Island, the upland is known as the Cape Breton Highlands. North Barren, a plateau that is the highest point in the province, is in the Cape Breton Highlands. Its altitude is 1,747 feet (532 meters) above sea level.

The coastal lowlands are valley regions that have been carved out of the Atlantic upland by centuries of wind and water erosion. They contain the province's agricultural regions. The most productive farmland is along the course of the Annapolis River, which runs southwestward between two upland plateaus near the Bay of Fundy. Other agricultural regions include the marshes along the Fundy coast, the flatlands around Chignecto

THE COMMUNITY SCHOOL
St. Louis, Mo.
Fifth Grade Library

Autumn adds blazing colors to the evergreen of pines in Cape Breton Highlands National Park. More than three-quarters of the province is covered with hardwood and softwood forest.

Bay—where Nova Scotia joins New Brunswick—and Minas Basin, just east of Chignecto Bay. These fertile lowlands are on the western side of the province, protected from the sea.

Both the mainland and the island contain deposits of many resources, including coal, gypsum, limestone, iron ore, barite, rock salt, sand, and gravel. Mining has long been an important part of the provincial economy.

Waterways

The economic and strategic importance of the sea has shaped much of Nova Scotia's history. The fishing banks off the coast of southeastern Canada attracted commercial fleets from Europe centuries ago, and this led to settlement and colonization. Through the Cabot Strait and the Gulf of St. Lawrence, the Europeans reached the St. Lawrence River and thus the interior of Canada. But fresh water has also been important in Nova Scotia's development.

More than 1,023 square miles (2,650 square kilometers) of the province is covered with rivers and lakes. These bodies of fresh water were helpful to the early settlers, serving as waterways into the interior. Today they are sources of hydroelectric power and transportation routes for the logging and mining industries.

Most of the province's rivers are less than 50 miles (80 kilometers) long. The longest rivers, the Mersey and the St. Mary's, are both 72 miles (116 kilometers) long and empty into the Atlantic from the south coast of the mainland. The Annapolis and Shubenacadie rivers irrigate the rich farmland of the Annapolis Valley. Some rivers, such as the St. Mary's, are known for their delicious fish, especially salmon. Others are powerful enough to provide hydroelectricity when dammed.

The waters of many of Nova Scotia's rivers rise and fall with the sea tides. This means that they can carry salt water inland, damaging crops. Since the earliest days of settlement, Nova Scotians have constructed sturdy and ingenious systems of locks and dikes to protect their agricultural land from salt contamination.

Nova Scotia has more than 3,000 lakes. Most of them are quite small, but the largest, a saltwater lake called Bras d'Or, covers 360 square miles (932 square kilometers) on Cape Breton Island, almost cutting the island in half. Lake Rossignol, the peninsula's largest lake, is located in the southeast. Like many of Nova Scotia's waterways, Lake Rossignol serves both economic and recreational purposes. It is a center of logging activities as well as a haven for swimmers and boaters.

Forests

Nova Scotia was once completely forested; about 77 percent of the province is still covered with forest. A wide variety of tree species grow in Nova Scotia, including 10 kinds of native softwoods, such as white pine, spruce, and balsam fir. Nearly a quarter of Nova Scotia's hardwood forest consists of yellow birch, but at least 13 other hardwoods grow there as well.

Most of the province's wildlife lives in its forests. The white-tailed deer is the most common large animal. Other species include black bears, moose, and wildcats. Early settlers earned their livelihood by hunting and trapping fur-bearing animals, such as beavers, minks, muskrats, raccoons, otters, and red foxes; these species still inhabit the forests and waterways. Marine life includes cod, haddock, flounder, herring, mackerel, swordfish, trout, lobsters, scallops, and oysters.

The province's many swamps are filled with mosses, lichens, and scrub heaths. Blueberry, bracken, raspberry, and sweet fern plants are also found. In the spring, the valleys and hillsides are painted in bright hues by many types of wildflowers. Especially abundant is the trailing arbutus, or mayflower, which was proclaimed the official provincial flower in 1901. Two wild plants that have been transplanted from Scotland are heather and purple thistle; these are greatly prized by the province's many residents of Scottish descent.

Low tide in the Bay of Fundy. The tides here are the world's highest—the water rises and falls more than 50 feet (15 meters) twice each day. At high tide the rocky crag in the background will appear to be nothing more than a tiny islet.

Climate

Nova Scotia's weather is as closely linked to the sea as its history and economy. The province is located at the intersection of two powerful ocean currents: the Labrador Current, which brings cold water south from the Arctic Ocean, and the Gulf Stream, which brings warm water north from the Gulf of Mexico. In summer, the mingling of the warm and cold currents produces a great deal of sea fog, which creeps in from the Bay of Fundy to cover the land in a blanket of heavy mist, sometimes for days at a stretch.

Apart from producing fog, the sea currents tend to moderate the province's weather. Nova Scotia's temperatures are far less extreme than those of inland Canada. The average January temperature is about 23 degrees Fahrenheit (-5 degrees Celsius) in most of the province. Only along the north coast are the temperatures severe, hovering around 5°F (-15°C) during the winter months.

Summer temperatures rarely go far above 74°F (56°C). Along the coast, June and July are very foggy and rather cool. The inland regions, however, have warm, sunny days and fairly high temperatures.

Rainfall in the province is heaviest along the Atlantic coast. Annual snowfall is about 90 inches (229 centimeters) per year in the Atlantic upland and about 60 to 80 inches (150 to 200 centimeters) in the coastal lowlands.

The History

In 1812, near Yarmouth harbor on the southwest corner of Nova Scotia's mainland, a group of archaeologists discovered an unusual stone. It was covered with carvings that formed runes, angular letters similar to those used in the alphabet of the ancient Norse peoples. Because the stone resembles Norse cemetery headstones, many scholars believe that it was left in Nova Scotia by Viking explorers in the 10th century A.D. Other historians, however, suggest that the stone is much older, perhaps dating back to the 2nd century B.C., and that it is a relic of ancient Basque adventurers who sailed to the New World. But whether it is of Basque or Norse origin, the stone is evidence that Europeans had visited the North American coast long before the official expeditions of Britain and France arrived to claim the region for their kings.

Jutting far into the Atlantic, Nova Scotia was a landfall for many European explorers in the 15th and 16th centuries. John Cabot, an Italian navigator in the service of Britain, had sailed west in search of a sea route to Asia. He did not find such a passage, but instead he discovered Nova Scotia. Around 1497 he

Opposite: French explorer Jacques Cartier (1491–1557) sailed into the Gulf of St. Lawrence in 1534 and claimed the land around it for France, paving the way for the French exploration and settlement of Atlantic Canada.
Above: Several Micmac and a missionary outside a Micmac wigwam in the 19th century. The Micmac, the Native American inhabitants of much of North America's east coast, were killed or driven onto reserves by European settlers.

landed on the southern mainland and then sailed up the coast to Cape Breton Island. Although Cabot claimed all the land he saw for King Henry VII of England, he left no settlers to occupy the territory. The British would not begin to settle along the Canadian coast for nearly two centuries.

Other European explorers followed Cabot's route across the Atlantic. Most of them were also searching for the hoped-for Northwest Passage to the Orient. In 1534, French navigator Jacques Cartier sailed into the Cabot Strait, stopping on Prince Edward Island. He then sailed across the Gulf of St. Lawrence to Quebec's Gaspé Peninsula. There he planted a cross and the flag of France, claiming all the land he saw—including what is now Nova Scotia—in the name of King Francis I of France.

France and Britain had claimed the same territory, but neither country had much interest in developing permanent settlements there. Both countries were much more interested in extracting valuable resources and shipping them back to Europe. The British concentrated on the fur trade, which eventually took them deep into the interior of the continent. The French, on the other hand, focused largely on the coastal fishery. It is now thought that French fishermen had been making regular visits to the offshore fishing banks of Canada as early as the 14th century, setting up temporary shore camps for drying their catches of codfish. This activity intensified after Cartier's voyage.

The Natives

Nova Scotia was not uninhabited when the Europeans arrived. The province's original inhabitants were the Micmac, Native Americans whose language belonged to the Algonquian language family, which also included the languages spoken by the Native peoples of New England and New York. Numbering about 20,000 in the 15th and 16th centuries, the Micmac lived in coastal communities from present-day Massachusetts to Quebec. They had inhabited the region for many centuries; in fact, some of their campsites in Nova Scotia are more than 5,000 years old.

The Micmac had a highly developed society. They lived in small communities along bays and rivers, in homes made primarily of animal skins. They were not farmers; instead, they hunted and fished for their food. Most Micmac clans migrated twice each year, moving into the forest to hunt deer and other game during the winter and then moving to the coast to fish during the summer. Their arts included painting and music. Fine crafts, such as elaborate stitchery and beadwork, also flourished.

The Micmac's traditional way of life was destroyed when large numbers of Europeans began settling in the region. As more and more French and British settlers arrived, the Micmac were eventually pushed off of their ancestral land and forced to move onto reservations. No longer able to range widely in search of game and fish, they attempted unsuccessfully to become farmers. Many Micmac died of starvation or were killed by European diseases such as smallpox and measles, against which they had no immunity. About 5,000 Micmacs remain in Nova Scotia today; most of them live in reserves on Cape Breton Island.

Viking longships probably coasted along Nova Scotia's shores in the 10th century. Some scholars believe that Cape Breton Island may have been the Markland, or Wooded Land, mentioned in the Norse sagas.

The French Years

The French name for their new territory in southeastern Canada was L'Acadie. The origin of the name is unknown, but it probably came from the ancient Greek word *Arcadia*, which was a mythical paradise of fruitful land and gentle weather. The *r* was dropped and the region became known as L'Acadie in French or Acadia in English. According to another theory, *acadie* was a word in the Micmac language that was adopted by the French as a place name.

The exact boundaries of Acadia have never been clearly defined. At first it included almost the entire east coast of Canada and part of the state of Maine in the United States. Eventually, however, the term was used mainly to refer to present-day Nova Scotia and New Brunswick.

The first attempt to settle Acadia was made in 1605 by the French. King Henry IV gave two explorers, Pierre du Guast and Samuel de Champlain, a charter to found a colony. They sailed along the Nova Scotia coast in 1604, making the first accurate map of the region, and then landed at Île de St. Croix, a small island in the mouth of the St. Croix River on the border between New Brunswick and Maine.

John Cabot and his son Sebastian, Italian navigators in the pay of the British, landed in Nova Scotia in 1497 and claimed it for King Henry VII. In this imaginative rendering of the landing, bears look on from a nearby cliff top.

The following summer, the French settlers moved the capital of Acadia to Port Royal, located on the southwest coast of present-day Nova Scotia. Soon they were joined by other French settlers. The capital of Acadia later shifted from time to time, depending on the military and political status of the region; at different periods it was located at Fredericton, New Brunswick, and Halifax and Louisbourg, both in Nova Scotia.

Nova Scotia's first French settlers, known as Acadians, developed a close-knit society, with their own traditions, customs, and language (a dialect based on French). They were an independent and hardy people who hunted, fished, and farmed. Against the French government's orders, they occasionally traded with the British colonists to the south, in what became the United States.

The Fight for Acadia

The French were the first to colonize Nova Scotia, but Britain also asserted its claim to the region. British colonists from New England, many of whom had been fishing in Acadian waters for decades, also set their sights on this territory. In the early 17th century, almost as soon as it was founded, Acadia came under assault from both Britain and New England. The first to attack the sparsely populated French colony were the New Englanders. In 1613, an expedition led by Sir Samuel Argall plundered Port Royal, chasing its inhabitants into the wilderness and burning the settlement to the ground. For years afterward, New Englanders considered Acadia an extension of New England; at times it was officially annexed to Massachusetts.

In 1621, King James I of Britain gave Acadia to a Scottish nobleman, Sir William Alexander. In honor of his homeland, Alexander renamed the territory New Scotland (or Nova Scotia in Latin). A new order of knights was founded, called the Barons of Nova Scotia, and Alexander gave each baron part of his land grant. A settlement was established, but it soon failed; most of the Scottish settlers went home in 1632 after a European treaty gave control of Nova Scotia to France. In 1713, however, the

In 1745, a British naval squadron from New York attacked the French on Cape Breton Island and placed the fortress of Louisbourg under siege. Nova Scotia passed back and forth between the British and the French many times during the 17th and 18th centuries.

A View of the Landing the New England Forces in ye Expedition against CAPE BRETON, 1745.

Treaty of Utrecht returned the mainland peninsula of Nova Scotia to Britain, leaving Cape Breton Island, Prince Edward Island, and present-day New Brunswick under French rule. After 1713, the French built a garrison on the southeast coast of Cape Breton Island and called it Louisbourg; it was one of France's largest and strongest fortresses in North America.

By the 1720s, Louisbourg had become a fortified city. It was not only the continent's fourth busiest port (after Boston, New York, and Philadelphia) but also the center of the French fishing industry. Strategically, Louisbourg was valuable as a first line of defense against attacks on Quebec and other parts of French Canada. By the 1740s, more than 2,000 people lived in the fort.

When another European war broke out in 1744, the French and British were adversaries once again. After news of the war reached Louisbourg, the fort's troops attacked the British fishing village of Canso, across the strait that separates Cape Breton Island from the mainland. A Royal British Navy squadron from New York, numbering some 4,500 men, arrived in the spring of 1745 to retaliate. Louisbourg was placed under siege, and the

French were forced to surrender within a few days. The British founded the city of Halifax on the mainland in 1749 and sent more than 4,000 colonists there from England and Scotland.

The Expulsion of the Acadians

Acadia—that is, the region comprising Nova Scotia and New Brunswick—was controlled by Britain after the middle of the 18th century. Most of the people who lived there, however, were Acadians of French descent. The ruling British, fearing that the Acadians would attack on France's behalf, ordered them to take an oath of loyalty to the British government. The Acadians refused, but they did promise to remain neutral in the seemingly endless struggle between France and Britain. This compromise was accepted for a short period of time. But when France regained some territory in nearby Newfoundland, the British

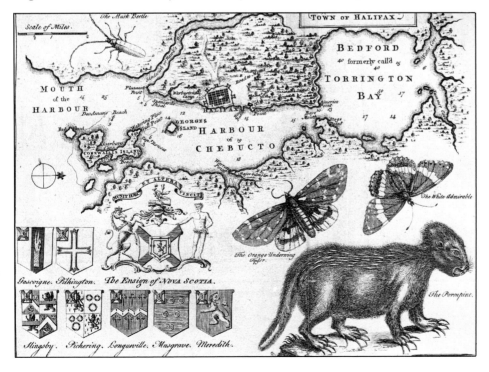

A 1750 map of Halifax shows the harbor, the newly founded British capital, and some fanciful depictions of local wildlife, including an unrealistically rendered porcupine. North is to the right.

decided to subjugate the Acadians. They moved the capital of Nova Scotia from Port Royal to Halifax, which had a large number of British inhabitants. Then they brought more British settlers into the territory. Some 7,000 British colonists, mostly from New England, arrived in Nova Scotia between 1750 and 1760.

The final blow against the Acadians came in 1755. The British seized Fort Beauséjour, an Acadian stronghold on the Isthmus of Chignecto, and attempted to make prisoners of the entire Acadian population. All of the Acadians who could be rounded up were expelled from their homes and deported to Britain or to British colonies. Some managed to escape the roundup and fled to Quebec or hid in isolated parts of Acadia. Many of them made their way to the French colony in Louisiana, where their descendants, the Cajuns, still preserve some aspects of Acadian culture.

Under British Rule

In 1763, the Treaty of Paris ended French rule in Canada. Prince Edward Island and Cape Breton Island became part of the Nova Scotia colony; Prince Edward Island, however, was made a

Acadian settlers weeping on the shore as they are forced onto ships that will carry them away from their homes. One of the saddest and most dramatic episodes in the province's history was the expulsion of the Acadians by the British in the 1750s. The event was commemorated in the poem *Evangeline,* by American poet Henry Wadsworth Longfellow.

separate colony six years later. Britain granted free land to colonists in the hope of expanding settlement in these territories, and immigrants from Scotland, Ireland, and the Yorkshire region of northern England began arriving in Nova Scotia.

In the latter part of the 18th century, as Britain and its American colonies drew closer to the revolutionary war, Nova Scotia became a bone of contention between the two parties. The American colonists wanted Nova Scotia and its fishing grounds to be part of their territory. They sent settlers to the colony and sometimes attacked it. The British, on the other hand, were determined to keep Nova Scotia separate from the New England colonies.

A large group of settlers from Massachusetts arrived in Nova Scotia in 1762. Many of them were disgusted by the harshness of British rule in the American colonies and hoped to find some measure of independence in Nova Scotia. During the American Revolution, some of these settlers sympathized with the rebels and attacked British posts in Nova Scotia.

A different type of settler came to Nova Scotia from New England during and after the American Revolution (1775–83). Approximately 35,000 United Empire Loyalists—New England colonists who remained loyal to Britain and did not want to remain in the independent United States—came to Nova Scotia in this period. Shelburne, on the south shore of the mainland, and Sydney, on the northeast shore of Cape Breton Island, were founded by Loyalists.

The third group of settlers who came to Nova Scotia from New England were Canada's first black residents. Some were the slaves of the Loyalists; others were blacks from the American colonies who had fought on the side of the British.

After the American Revolution and influx of settlers from the American colonies, Nova Scotia's population was so large that its inhabitants urged the Colonial Office in London to divide the colony into several smaller sections. This was completed in 1784, making New Brunswick, Cape Breton Island, and Nova Scotia into separate colonies. Cape Breton Island was reunited with Nova Scotia in 1820.

Over the years, Nova Scotia's most prosperous eras have been in times of war. Its location in the Atlantic makes it a good site for strategic military bases and an efficient shipping point for war supplies, including the region's own lumber, coal, and fish. The War of 1812, between Britain and the United States, ushered Nova Scotia into its first economic boom. Britain invested in its defenses, building military bases in Halifax and Canso. The products of Nova Scotia's farmers, fishermen, and lumberjacks were in great demand and were used to supply the armies of Britain and its allies.

The population of Nova Scotia rose along with its fortunes. In 1820, when Cape Breton was reunited with Nova Scotia, the population of the colony was about 28,000. By mid-century, 55,000 new colonists had arrived, most of them Scottish or Irish. The Scots continued to emigrate to Nova Scotia throughout the century, establishing themselves as the largest ethnic group on Cape Breton Island. People began mining coal and gypsum and farming the rich soil around the Bay of Fundy and in the Annapolis Valley. Trade with other colonies and countries expanded.

Confederation

Political changes accompanied the economic development that occurred in Nova Scotia during the early 19th century. During the mid-1830s, a dynamic statesman and newspaper editor named Joseph Howe led a campaign for responsible government—that is, government in which decisions would be made by the elected representatives. Howe was a careful and conservative reformer who pressed for change through more than a decade of quiet but persistent negotiations. Finally, in 1848, Nova Scotia became the first completely self-governing colony in the British Empire. James Uniacke, the son of an Irish lawyer, was its premier; Howe was secretary of the colony.

The new government wanted to complete a railway that would connect Nova Scotia with the colonies of Canada West

(Ontario) and Canada East (Quebec), thereby increasing trade with these large and wealthy colonies. Howe, who took the post of chief railway commissioner, was unable to achieve that goal, but he did oversee the construction of a railway within the province. Lines from Halifax to both Windsor and Truro were completed in 1854.

During this period, Britain's other Canadian colonies were also growing in population and economic strength. Colonists began to talk about joining together in a union, or confederation. Such a confederation would create a larger, more powerful state that could resist invasion—Nova Scotia especially feared the increasingly powerful United States, its enemy since the early days of colonization.

Perhaps more important than military security, however, was the increased political and economic power that confederation would bring; the smaller and poorer colonies could benefit greatly by becoming part of a larger confederation with extensive resources. Nova Scotia first proposed that it be reunited with New Brunswick, thereby doubling its population and economic strength. Next the three Maritime Provinces discussed the possibility of a union. But before a decision on a maritime union could be made, Canada West and Canada East suggested a united Canada. In Nova Scotia, Joseph Howe, no longer a member of government, fought against confederation. Instead of looking westward and inland, Howe claimed, Nova Scotia should strengthen its special position as the center of trade and shipping on the Atlantic seaboard. In addition, he indicated that Nova Scotia shared more cultural and economic qualities with Britain and the other Maritime Provinces than with Quebec, which was largely French, or with Ontario, which was far away and unconcerned with maritime issues.

Charles Tupper, who was elected premier of Nova Scotia in 1864, stood in favor of confederation. At odds with Howe, Tupper felt that Nova Scotia's coal, lumber, and manufacturing industries would benefit from a Canadian union, especially if a railway—promised by Canada East and Canada West as a condition of Confederation—linked Halifax with Montreal.

Nova Scotian statesman Joseph Howe guided the province's development from the 1830s to the 1850s. Due to his efforts, Great Britain permitted Nova Scotia to govern itself; it was the first British colony to do so.

As premier, Tupper did not have to put the matter to a vote. He had the power to decide the issue on his own. So Nova Scotia joined Quebec, Ontario, and New Brunswick in the Confederation, which formed the new Dominion of Canada on July 1, 1867. Historians agree that if the people of Nova Scotia had voted on the matter, Confederation would have been soundly defeated, for at least 65 percent of the population opposed it. Many times in the decades after Confederation, Nova Scotia tried to secede from Canada. Although these attempts failed, they created lingering tensions between the federal and provincial governments.

The 20th Century

The years following Confederation were difficult ones for Nova Scotia and for Atlantic Canada in general. Several political and economic factors combined to undermine Nova Scotia's economy. Its once-booming shipbuilding industry collapsed as iron-hulled

Coal and shipping were the mainstays of the economy in the late 19th and early 20th centuries. Coaling teams competed to see who could load the most coal in the least time. According to their sign, this 1901 coaling party for the ship *Indefatigable* loaded 403 tons in 5½ hours.

Charred timber and mounds of rubble were all that remained of the Halifax waterfront after a French munitions ship exploded in the harbor in 1917, destroying half the city. The Halifax disaster was the largest man-made explosion before the atomic bomb.

ships replaced wooden ones. At the same time, trade with the United States, a prime trading partner, was dealt a devastating blow in the late 1860s. The United States placed stiff tariffs, or import taxes, on goods made in Canada and sold in the United States; this made Nova Scotia's fish, lumber, and coal too costly for many of the province's American customers.

In some ways, the Maritime Provinces were left behind as the Dominion of Canada grew and prospered. Central Canada's vast wheat fields produced grain exports that soon became far more valuable to the nation than any of the goods produced in Atlantic Canada, and the west coast port of Vancouver opened the way for increased trade with the nations of the Pacific Rim. As a result, federal attention and support slowly shifted westward, to the prairie provinces and the Pacific coast. The government did build the promised railway linking Nova Scotia with Quebec and the rest of Canada, but shipping goods to and from Nova Scotia by rail was very costly, so the railroad actually did little to boost the province's economy.

Nova Scotia prospered again during World War I (1914–18), when Halifax was the headquarters of the Allied fleets in the North Atlantic Ocean. Wartime demand for iron, steel, fish, and lumber revitalized the province's sagging economy. Yet the war also brought tragedy to Nova Scotia. In 1917, a French military supply ship loaded with munitions exploded in Halifax Harbor. The blast killed about 2,000 people and destroyed at least half of the capital city. Halifax was rebuilt, but the city still bears some of the scars from the Great Explosion.

Nova Scotia was home to Canada's first significant black population, and many blacks live there today. Tensions between blacks and whites in the schools and elsewhere during the 1980s led to an examination of racism in the province.

After the war, Nova Scotia once again fell into an economic depression. The economies of Prince Edward Island and New Brunswick were also suffering, and out of these hard times a movement for "Maritime rights" emerged. The spokespeople for Maritime rights demanded a decrease in freight rates and an increase in federal aid to their provincial economies. They made some gains, but economic and social development in Atlantic Canada continued to lag behind that of the rest of the country.

A Nova Scotia politician named Angus Macdonald attempted to improve conditions after he was elected premier in 1933. Although he did not succeed in getting the federal government to pass reforms, Macdonald did form one of the most effective provincial governments in Nova Scotia's history. Even during the Great Depression of the 1930s, when Nova Scotia's economic condition was at its worst, he and his Liberal party were able to introduce a number of social reforms, including old age pensions and unemployment benefits.

World War II (1939–45) brought another boom. Once again, Halifax became the major port for shipping munitions, troops, and supplies from North America to western Europe. During the 1950s, Nova Scotia was able to utilize some of the capital it had amassed during the war, combined with large grants of federal money, to bring about much-needed changes. Schools were expanded, highways constructed, and industries developed. Despite this burst of growth, however, Nova Scotia was still struggling to keep its economy alive. A new surge of federal funding in the 1960s brought a host of programs and agencies intended to promote economic growth. Unfortunately, two of the province's leading industries, coal mining and steel making, suffered severe losses during this period, when the worldwide demand for their products declined.

In the late 1980s, Nova Scotian economists and politicians began to hope that 2 energy-related activities could lift the province out of its 40-year decline. In an effort to reduce the need for expensive imported oil, Nova Scotia has begun to revive its dormant coal industry, increasing employment in the province, especially on Cape Breton Island. Plans are also underway to extract oil and natural gas from the undersea reserves off Sable Island, adding new resources to Nova Scotia's economic base.

Always a strong and determined people, Nova Scotians face the 21st century with optimism, despite their history of economic struggle in the 20th century. In fact, concerns about the province's future have prompted Nova Scotians to debate the rate at which the resource industries should be allowed to grow. Although everyone concurs that there is a strong need for economic development, many Nova Scotians are determined to preserve their province's natural beauty and traditional way of life.

The Economy

Nova Scotia's economic development has been hampered by several factors, including the province's distance from the large cities and markets of central Canada, its lack of investment capital, and federal policies that, according to many eastern Canadians, favor the central and western provinces. Nova Scotia's economy has traditionally depended on its four resource-based primary industries: agriculture, fishing, mining, and forestry. But the failure of this economy to meet the needs of the 20th century has resulted in the province having one of Canada's lowest per capita incomes and highest unemployment rates.

The province's economy is changing, however. As in most industrialized nations and regions, service and financial industries now make up the majority of Nova Scotia's gross domestic product (GDP, the sum of all goods and services produced in the province). Education, health care, engineering, legal services, and financial institutions account for more than 75 percent of the GDP and employ about two-thirds of the province's workers.

Opposite: A German container ship is loaded with cargo. Nova Scotia's seaports handle trade to and from all parts of the world.
Above: Blueberry harvest at Oxford, near the Isthmus of Chignecto.

Finance and tourism are two important sectors of the province's economy. The Bank of Nova Scotia is one of the largest in Canada, and the capital city of Halifax is a leading Canadian center of international trade. The tourism industry currently employs about 27,000 people. More than 1 million people visit Nova Scotia every year, and the money they spend adds millions of dollars of revenue to the provincial income. Manufacturing has also increased in importance during the 20th century, and the primary industries continue to contribute to the GDP.

Manufacturing

Manufacturing is the second largest sector of Nova Scotia's economy, after the service industries. It accounts for about 14 percent of the GDP. About 47,000 people are employed in the province's 800 plants. Most of these are small plants, which process such local products as pulpwood, fruit, and vegetables. Food processing, especially the production of fish products, is the largest component of the manufacturing sector. Dozens of fish-processing plants are scattered along the coast of Nova Scotia. Second in importance is the manufacture of paper products, primarily newsprint (the paper that newspapers are printed on) and cardboard. Chemicals, petroleum products, steel, tires, and transportation equipment are also manufactured. Among the biggest plants are two factories operated by Michelin Tires Limited near Bridgewater and New Glasgow and a government-owned steel mill in Sydney. At least half of all the province's manufactured products are exported, and more than 65 percent of all exports go to the United States.

Mining and Energy

By 1990, the mining industry and the search for energy sources had become more important to Nova Scotia's economy than they had been at any time since the 1950s, accounting for about two

A salt mine in Pugwash on the Northumberland Strait. The province also has reserves of coal, iron ore, gypsum, limestone, oil, and natural gas. Gold was mined in the early 20th century, but the gold mines are played out.

percent of the annual GDP. Approximately 6,300 people are employed in extracting coal, gypsum, salt, sand, and stone from Nova Scotia's mines and quarries.

Nova Scotia has been a leading producer of gypsum, a mineral used in the construction industry, since the 1780s. One of the world's largest gypsum deposits is located at Windsor, and the mineral is found in almost all of the province's 18 counties. More than 70 percent of the gypsum that is extracted is sold to the United States; the income generated, therefore, rises and falls according to shifts in the U.S. construction industry.

Coal is by far the province's most important mineral. The largest and most productive coal mines are located on Cape Breton Island, although some coal is mined in Pictou County on the mainland as well. During the early 20th century, coal was vital to the province's economy and to its domestic industry—in addition to exporting coal, Nova Scotia used it to provide fuel for ships and for homes and factories. The mines were among the province's biggest employers. Then, during the 1950s and 1960s, Nova Scotia—like the rest of the industrialized world—began to

Nova Scotia is Christmas tree country. Each year, thousands of evergreens from Nova Scotian tree farms are exported for the Christmas season to markets in Canada and the United States.

rely upon oil and gas, which were abundant and inexpensive. This source of energy did not remain stable for very long; when the OPEC oil cartel raised its prices in the early 1970s, Nova Scotia found it difficult to buy enough oil and gas to meet its needs, but its coal mining industry had fallen into decline.

Since the 1970s, the province has made a determined and successful effort to reduce its dependency on foreign oil by reviving its coal mining industry. By 1990, coal was providing about 77 percent of Nova Scotia's electrical needs, up from 23 percent in 1980. Hydroelectric plants supply the rest of the province's power. The first tidal power plant developed in North America operates at the mouth of the Annapolis River; it uses the largest turbine ever built for hydroelectric development. The province's decreased dependency on foreign oil, however, may have a price; many environmentalists have become concerned about the long-term ecological effects of mining and burning coal in large quantities.

The quest for energy sources has led to offshore exploration for gas and oil, especially near Sable Island. In March 1982, Nova Scotia's premier, John Buchanan, signed a 42-year agreement with Canada's federal government that allows offshore development and gives the province a large share of the profits.

Forestry

Forestry has been an essential part of Nova Scotia's economy for many years. During the 19th century, some of the world's finest sailing ships were made of timber from Nova Scotia's forests. The forests are still harvested. Hardwood forestry focuses on yellow birch, red maple, and sugar maple, which are made into lumber. Softwood forestry concentrates on balsam fir. These are used in the pulp-and-paper industry, which is now larger than the lumber industry. Nova Scotia's abundance of balsam fir produces thousands of Christmas trees that are exported to other Canadian provinces and to the United States each year. Lunenburg County on the Atlantic coast is sometimes called the Christmas Tree Capital of the World.

About 77 percent of Nova Scotia is forested. In many parts of Canada, forests are owned and monitored by the federal government, but three-quarters of Nova Scotia's forest land is privately owned. As a result, although there are some large-scale forestry operations, Nova Scotia has a greater share of small-scale lumbering companies than the other provinces. Most forestry operations are located along the rivers.

Fishing

The fishing industry, which drew the first European settlers from across the ocean, now accounts for only two percent of the GDP. Yet in Canada, Nova Scotia is second only to British Columbia in the value of its fishery. Nearly 15,000 fishermen and about 9,300 onshore workers are employed in the fishing and fish-processing industries.

The waters around Nova Scotia have been fished for centuries, not only by Canada but also by other seafaring nations as well. Control of the North Atlantic fishing grounds has been in dispute since the 1500s. In 1977, fearing that the fish reserves were being dangerously depleted by large commercial fleets from other countries, Canada declared a 200-mile (320-kilometer) fishing limit—in other words, Canada claimed sole ownership of

Lobstermen prepare their pots and lines for a day's work. Fishing—both close to the shore and on the fishing grounds farther from the coast—still makes an important contribution to the local economy.

the fishing grounds within this limit. The Canadian government hoped to regulate fishing in most of the productive fishing grounds on its continental shelf.

Enforcement of the limit, though, has been uneven—varying in strictures at different times and in different locations. Furthermore, many fishermen in Nova Scotia object to what they consider meddling and overregulation by the federal government. A strict quota system, which limits the size of the catch, has forced some of the larger fish-processing plants to operate at less than full capacity. This in turn means that they have to raise their prices and lay off some of their employees.

In 1984, the United States contested Canadian ownership of Georges Bank, one of the world's richest fishing areas, located just south of Nova Scotia. In the settlement, Canada received one-sixth of the disputed territory, but this was the most valuable portion. Fishermen in New England were aggrieved.

Agriculture

About 10 percent of Nova Scotia is productive agricultural land. The largest cultivated area is the Annapolis Valley, which produces about one-third of Nova Scotia's fruit and vegetable crops and is best known for its magnificent apple orchards, although vegetables and potatoes are becoming important crops as well. Small family farms are common throughout the province; communities often survive on a combination of fishing and farming. Dairy farming, poultry and hog raising, and cattle ranching are also economically significant.

Because fertile land is scarce in Nova Scotia, the province's first European settlers, the Acadians, devised a way to expand the region's farmland. They built dikes and dams to drain the marshes near the Bay of Fundy. In recent years, the province's Marshlands Reclamation Commission has preserved and extended the Acadians' remarkably effective system of dikes.

Nova Scotia is known for its fine apple harvest in the Annapolis Valley. Most agricultural operations are small family-owned farms or orchards.

The People

The Scotsman, clad in his kilt and playing the bagpipes, is the most enduring symbol of the Nova Scotian people. At one time, the Scots outnumbered all other ethnic groups in the province. Thousands of both Protestant and Roman Catholic Scots, forced to leave their country because of famine and political persecution in the early 19th century, settled in New Scotland. They found the colony, with its rocky crags and rugged coastline, strikingly similar to Scotland, and they transplanted many Scottish customs to their new homeland.

In the 1990s, the Scottish presence is still very visible in Nova Scotia. People of Scottish descent make up more than 25 percent of the province's total population of 873,199; some local historians claim that more clans, as Scottish extended family groupings are called, are represented in Nova Scotia than in Scotland. Many Nova Scotians of Scottish descent still speak Gaelic, the traditional language of their ancestors, and Scottish-style fairs and festivals are held throughout the province. These include the annual Gathering of the Clans and the Highland Games, which are modeled on traditional events in Scotland.

One quarter of the province's inhabitants are of Scottish descent, and many events celebrate Scottish heritage. At a Scottish festival in Antigonish, marchers provide traditional bagpipe music *(opposite)* and a participant in the Highland Games tries his arm in a test of strength *(above)*.

Nova Scotia's Acadian heritage is reflected in a statue of Evangeline, the Acadian heroine of Longfellow's poem, at Grand Pré National Historic Park, which also has a museum of Acadian artifacts and documents.

People of British descent—including Scottish, Irish, and English ethnic groups—account for about 73 percent of Nova Scotia's population. Irish immigrants arrived in great numbers during the mid-19th century, when Ireland was in the grip of a severe famine. But although the British influence is strong, it has never completely overpowered the influences of other ethnic and cultural groups. About 11 percent of the province's population consists of descendants of the French Acadian settlers. They live in many parts of Nova Scotia but are somewhat concentrated on the northeastern coast of Cape Breton. In small towns such as Chéticamp, Church Point, and Pubnico, most Acadians still speak the Acadian dialect of French that developed over decades of isolation from their home country. They share their language and customs with the public during festivals and celebrations held every year. There is also a substantial German-Canadian population in Nova Scotia. The German influence is most visible in and around the cities of New Germany, situated in the center of the peninsula, and Lunenburg, located on the south coast.

Blacks are another significant ethnic minority in the province. Most of the first black Nova Scotians were slaves who were brought north by the Loyalists in the late 18th century. Others were former slaves who had escaped from the American South and made their way north along the Underground Railroad. The institution of slavery was never well established in Nova Scotia and was outlawed altogether by the end of the 18th century.

Until the 1960s, blacks constituted approximately five percent of Nova Scotia's population; this percentage was higher than anywhere else in Canada. Since then, many blacks—and whites as well—have left the province to seek jobs elsewhere, especially in Toronto, Ontario. Nova Scotia now has a black population of about 15,000, or slightly less than 2 percent of the total population.

Nova Scotia's troubled economy has, in general, brought more hardship to the black residents of the province. Unemployment rates among blacks are about twice those of whites, and the average yearly income of black Nova Scotians is about half that of whites. Traditionally, blacks in Nova Scotia lived in segregated towns or in parts of cities that lagged behind other areas in terms of social services and the quality of life. Most blacks in Halifax, for example, lived in a slum called Africaville until it was razed as part of an urban renewal program in the 1960s.

Tensions between the province's blacks and whites have often run high, especially during slumps in the economy. In 1989, the tension erupted into violence when a fistfight between a black student and a white student turned into a full-scale brawl involving 30 or more students at a high school near Halifax. The black community accused the school system of widespread racism; an investigation into both the fight and the larger issue of racism was still underway in early 1991.

Another Nova Scotian minority, the Micmac Native Americans, also claims that racism is a serious problem in the province. Nova Scotia's judicial system came under attack when it was discovered that Donald Marshall, the son of the grand chief of the Micmac nation, had been wrongly convicted of murder in 1971. Marshall spent more than a decade in prison, and the Micmac claimed that the wrongful conviction was the result of racial prejudice against Natives. In 1987, a federal commission investigated the case and found that many—although certainly not all—of Nova Scotia's police officers and jurists were prejudiced against Natives.

These two disturbing incidents have caused Nova Scotians to examine and debate the question of racism and its effect on their communities. Most Nova Scotians like to think of themselves as warm and open people who, while proud of their heritage and their traditions, welcome immigrants from all over the world.

Education

In 1865, premier Charles Tupper enacted laws that instituted a public school system in Nova Scotia, offering free education to all children. In 1990 about 230,000 young Nova Scotians were attending the province's schools. Children are required to attend school between the ages of 6 and 16. If they wish to go on to college, they may attend 1 or more of the province's 11 degree-granting colleges and universities, some of which have international reputations. Most of these institutions of higher learning are small and are affiliated with a religious denomination.

The largest and most well known university is Dalhousie University, located on the outskirts of Halifax. Founded in 1818 as a nondenominational facility, Dalhousie has undergone a number of transformations. For a time it was run as a Presbyterian college that competed with an Anglican institution called King's College. Later it served as a local high school. Dalhousie now offers 100 degree and diploma programs in arts and sciences, management studies, and health professions. Its graduate programs in law, medical research, and ocean studies are renowned. Dalhousie has more than 8,000 full-time undergraduate and graduate students and shares a faculty with its former rival, King's College.

One unusual institution is the Gaelic College at St. Ann's, on Cape Breton Island, where the Gaelic language is taught and summer courses are given in Scottish subjects such as bagpipe playing and highland dancing. It is the only college of its kind in North America.

Dalhousie University in Halifax is the province's largest institution of higher learning. It was founded in 1818.

The Miner's Museum in Glace Bay is one of many local and regional specialty museums. Each deals with a different aspect of Nova Scotia's history, economy, or culture.

The Arts

Nova Scotia celebrates its history and traditions with historical museums and ethnic festivals that rival those of much larger provinces. It has so many seasonal and annual celebrations that it is sometimes called the Festival Province, and nearly every town has a historical museum. Some of these museums trace the province's history as a maritime center; others, such as the Miner's Museum in Glace Bay, exhibit relics of a particular industry or ethnic group. A museum at Grand Pré National Historic Park near Wolfville houses exhibits that recount the sad tale of the Acadian deportations.

Nova Scotia cherishes its past but also nurtures the contemporary arts. The province boasts a lively modern theater and a busy art community. The Neptune Theatre in Halifax was founded in the 1960s but took its name from the oldest theater in North America: During the first few hard winters in Acadia in the early 17th century, Samuel de Champlain produced theatrical performances to amuse the tired and lonely settlers and called his troupe the Neptune Theatre. Today's Neptune Theatre is one of the best-known professional theater groups in Atlantic Canada, performing musicals and dramas, both classical and modern.

Another professional theater company is the Mermaid Theatre of Wolfville. Actors and dancers in this troupe use giant puppets to enact folk tales, many of them based on Micmac stories. The art of puppetry has become a Nova Scotian specialty, and the Canadian Puppet Festival, held in Chester, Nova Scotia, includes puppet productions of classic fairy tales, folk tales, and ballets for audiences of all ages. Amateur theater groups exist in many towns throughout the province.

Music in Nova Scotia is dominated by Scottish bagpipe music, Irish jigs, and Acadian fiddle music. Folk music of all sorts is popular, and Nova Scotia has many talented folk performers. The Halifax Symphony Orchestra offers a program of classical music and also tours the Atlantic Provinces. There are many smaller chamber orchestras and choral groups. One well-known singing group is called Men of the Deeps. This choir of Cape Breton coal miners has performed throughout Canada, the United States, Europe, and China.

Nova Scotia has a number of small art museums and galleries. The Art Museum of Nova Scotia in Halifax was recently renovated and houses traveling exhibitions as well as permanent collections of European and local paintings and sculptures. Nova Scotia's best-known native-born artist is Thomas Forrestall, who was born in Middleton in 1936. His realistic paintings capture the beauty of the Atlantic landscape and depict the fishing villages and huts along the coast.

Many writers, past and present, have drawn upon the province's history, culture, and setting in their works. Nova Scotia's most important early writer was Thomas Haliburton (1796–1865), whose satirical stories about Sam Slick were very popular. Sam was a clockmaker with little respect for politicians or voters; his antics were commentaries on the political scene of the 1820s and 1830s. Traditional Nova Scotian life was portrayed in *The Mountain and the Valley* by Ernest Buckler and *The Channel Shore* by Charles Bruce. Contemporary writers of fiction whose works also comment on life in Nova Scotia are Chipman Hall (*Lightly*), Alistair MacLeod (*The Lost Salt Gift of Blood*), and Susan Kerslake (*Middlewatch*).

Recreation

Nova Scotians boast that hockey—Canada's favorite sport—was invented by soldiers stationed in Halifax in the 1800s. Whether or not the sport originated in Halifax, hockey is still a favorite of Nova Scotian athletes and fans alike. Although Nova Scotia does not have a National Hockey League team, it has produced NHL players such as Al MacInnis. Halifax is home to the Nova Scotia Voyageurs, the farm team of the NHL's Montreal Canadiens; the Voyageurs play at the world-class Metro Centre Stadium.

Nova Scotia offers many opportunities for amateur athletes as well. During the winter, cross-country skiing is popular throughout the province. In the summer, boaters, swimmers, and sunbathers flock to the beaches, especially on the Northumberland Strait, which has the warmest waters on the east coast of Canada.

The Northumberland Strait, which has the warmest water in the province, attracts swimmers and sunbathers during the summer.

The Cities

The Twin Cities

Founded within a year of each other, in 1749 and 1750, Halifax and Dartmouth are two of the largest cities in Atlantic Canada. Dartmouth is northeast of Halifax, across the harbor, and the two cities are joined by two suspension bridges. They have a combined population of nearly 179,000, forming Canada's largest urban center east of Montreal. The twin cities are the center of Nova Scotia's government, arts, education, health care, and business institutions.

Halifax is often called the Warden of the North because of its strategic military role in Canadian history. It was built as a balance to the French fort at Louisbourg when the battle between the French and the British for control of Atlantic Canada was at its peak. Halifax is filled with reminders of its military past. Most striking is the Halifax Citadel, an enormous star-shaped fort on a hill overlooking the harbor.

More than half the city was destroyed when a French munitions ship exploded in the harbor in 1917. A few of the old buildings that survived the Great Explosion are located in the

Opposite: Historic Properties is an enclave of old buildings on the Halifax waterfront that have been restored and converted into shops and restaurants.
Above: The Halifax skyline by night. Nova Scotia's capital has a population of about 114,000 and is the largest city in the province.

heart of the modern city, near the waterfront in a district called Historic Properties. Historic Properties consists of a dozen 17th- and 18th-century structures that have been converted into shops and restaurants.

Although Halifax was once distinctly Irish and English, it is now an ethnic mosaic. The Haligonians, as its residents are called, include blacks, Asians, and people from southern and eastern Europe.

Halifax's economy has long centered on trade, transportation, and finance. Its port is the largest in Atlantic Canada, and railway lines connect it to central Canadian markets. Also important to the city's economy are government administration, health services, and education centers, which employ a sizable number of Haligonians.

Like the province itself, Halifax is almost completely surrounded by water. It juts out into Bedford Basin, which separates it from Dartmouth.

Dartmouth was founded as an agricultural community to supply the colonial capital with produce, but it is now a city in its own right. Although it is closely tied to its larger neighbor both by bridges and by a shared economy, it has a characteristic atmosphere of its own.

Called the City of Lakes by its 65,000 residents, Dartmouth has 25 lakes within its city limits. These sparkling bodies of water enliven the cityscape of high-rise towers and industrial plants. Dartmouth is one of the fastest-growing residential and commercial centers in Atlantic Canada. The Burnside Industrial Park, which opened in 1968, is the largest such complex in the region, catering to the service and sales industries.

Dartmouth also has some of the region's most prestigious research organizations. The Bedford Institute of Oceanography is Canada's principal oceanographic center. Operated by the federal Department of the Fisheries, the institute performs long-term research in the marine sciences. The Nova Scotia Research Foundation Corporation, also located in Dartmouth, was established by the federal government in 1946 to explore opportunities for Nova Scotia's economic development. The

corporation has established world-renowned centers of research in ocean technology, biotechnology, and microtechnology.

Sydney

Sydney, Nova Scotia's third largest city, is located in northeastern Cape Breton. Known as the Steel Capital of Nova Scotia, Sydney has been a center of industrial activity in Atlantic Canada since 1899, when the Dominion Iron and Steel Company was established to extract coal from Cape Breton Island and iron ore from Newfoundland Island.

Sydney's first residents were Loyalists. They arrived in 1784, when Cape Breton was still a separate colony. Until 1820, when Cape Breton and the mainland were united, Sydney was the capital of the Cape Breton colony. Today, although the provincial government is in Halifax, Sydney remains the center of the island's business and government sectors.

Lunenburg, on the south coast, is both a center of German Canadian settlement and a picturesque fishing village that seems to represent the best of Nova Scotian tradition. The Nova Scotians are eager to boost their province's economy through further development of the tourism and energy industries—but not at the expense of Nova Scotia's natural beauty and traditional charm.

Most of Sydney's workers are employed by the coal or steel industries. The local port continues to serve the surrounding coal towns, and Sydney's railroad link to central Canada, built at the end of the 19th century, carries the city's products inland.

Chéticamp

With a population of about 3,000 people, this fishing village on the northern coast of Cape Breton Island is the heart of Nova Scotia's Acadian community. A few miles offshore is Chéticamp Island, where a group of Acadians who had been expelled from the mainland settled in 1755.

Set between the Cape Breton Highlands and the Gulf of St. Lawrence, Chéticamp survives today in much the same way it always has, as a fishing and farming center. The beauty of the village, and of Cape Breton in general, cannot compensate for the hardships most residents endure. Some of the province's highest unemployment rates and lowest standards of living are found in Cape Breton.

Tourism is a growing industry in Chéticamp and other villages. Many visitors to Chéticamp stop at Les Trois Pignons, an information center and museum that features Acadian arts and crafts. Of particular interest are the rugs and tapestries made in centuries-old Acadian styles. Elizabeth LeFort, a native of Chéticamp, is considered one of Canada's finest tapestry makers; her works hang in the Vatican, the White House, and Buckingham Palace.

Not far from Chéticamp is an entrance to Cape Breton Highlands National Park. Approximately 370 square miles (958 square kilometers) in area, the park stretches from the Gulf of St. Lawrence in the west to the Atlantic Ocean in the east and is home to some of the province's most abundant wildlife.

Fishermen weigh their catch of crabs on the docks of Chéticamp, one of many small fishing villages where Acadian culture and tradition remain alive.

Things to Do and See

Opposite: The Halifax Public Gardens are among the oldest landscaped gardens in North America.
Above: The Citadel, the star-shaped fort built by the British, commands a sweeping view of Halifax Harbor.

• **Citadel National Historic Park,** Halifax: The star-shaped fortress called the Citadel was built in 1828 on a hill above Halifax, on the site of fortifications dating back to the city's founding in 1749. The park, offering a splendid view of the city and harbor below, includes the fortress; the Army Museum, which depicts the history of colonial warfare; a gift shop; and a parade ground where kilted soldiers perform military drills.

• **Nova Scotia Museum,** Halifax: Exhibits depicting the wildlife and resources of Nova Scotia, including a "touch and feel" section for children, are the highlights of this museum. "Man and His Environment" is another noted permanent exhibit.

• **Black Cultural Center for Nova Scotia,** Halifax: A library, an auditorium, and several galleries provide forums for exhibits and lectures about black history and culture in the province.

• **Province House,** Halifax: Canada's oldest legislative building is still the seat of the provincial government. It contains a large library of materials about Nova Scotia's history.

• **Marine Museum of the Atlantic,** Halifax: A museum that traces the course of science and exploration in the North Atlantic. Among the exhibits is the ship *Acadia,* which was used by scientists to map the coasts of Labrador and the Canadian Arctic early in the 20th century.

• **Alexander Graham Bell National Historic Site,** Baddeck, Cape Breton Island: The world's most complete museum about the life and works of Alexander Graham Bell, the inventor of the telephone. It also houses the first airplane to fly in Canada.

• **Cape Breton Highlands National Park,** near Chéticamp: The park offers spectacular views of the island and the surrounding waters. The oldest national park in eastern Canada, the Highlands protects a variety of wildlife, including moose, bald eagles, hares, coyotes, bears, and bobcats. It is the largest remaining area of protected wilderness in the province.

• **Fortress Louisbourg,** Cape Breton Island: Canada's most ambitious historical restoration has created a replica of the fortress and homes of Louisbourg as they looked in 1750. The site has an interpretive center that describes the long and complicated French and British war in the region.

• **Miner's Museum,** Springhill: Experienced miners guide interested tourists down into a working coal mine. The nearby museum depicts the mine's dramatic history, including a disaster that claimed 125 lives in 1891 and a rockfall that killed 39 people in 1956.

• **Geological, Mineral, and Gem Museum,** Parrsboro: Highlights of this museum include a collection of local minerals, gems, fossils, and geological maps and a rockhound field where visitors can search for treasures of their own.

The *Bluenose II*, a replica of a championship sailing and fishing vessel, provides coastal tours.

• **La Vieille Maison,** Meteghan: A restored house displays artifacts from 19th-century Acadian life on the shores of St. Mary's Bay. Features include original documents, period furniture, and Acadian guides in costume.

• **Fisheries Museum of the Atlantic,** Lunenburg: This museum features displays about the way of life of Canada's Atlantic fishermen, the equipment and vessels they have used, and the marine life of the area. Two authentic fishing vessels are also on display.

• **Kejimkujik National Park:** Located in the west-central part of the mainland, the park is 238 square miles (281 square kilometers) of wilderness dotted with lakes and crisscrossed with streams and rivers—a canoeist's or camper's paradise.

• **Shubenacadie Provincial Wildlife Park,** Shubenacadie: Fifty acres (20 hectares) of natural woodland, containing many species of North American birds and animals.

The Cabot Trail winds for 172 miles (278 kilometers) in a loop around the northwestern tip of Cape Breton Island. It is said to be one of the most beautiful drives in North America.

Festivals & Holidays

Canada Day Celebrations, throughout the province: In towns and villages all over Nova Scotia, the birth of the Canadian nation is celebrated on July 1 with fireworks, parades, barbecues, and concerts.

Annapolis Valley Apple Blossom Festival, Annapolis Valley: One of the biggest events in the province takes place every year at the end of May and features barbecues, sports, art shows, teas, dances, concerts, fireworks, a parade, and the crowning of the year's Apple Blossom Queen.

Blessing of the Fleet, Meteghan, Main-a-Dieu, Petit-de-Grat, and other Acadian villages: Following a centuries-old tradition, fishing boats are blessed at the start of the fishing season in May and June.

Cabot Pageant, Cape North: A pageant held every year at the end of June reenacts the landing of explorer John Cabot on Nova Scotia's shores in 1497.

Nova Scotia International Tattoo, Halifax: A tattoo is a military drill held outdoors to music, and this one, held at the beginning of July, opens the International Gathering of the Clans, a yearly reunion of Scottish clans. Bagpipers, military bands, and Scottish dancers perform throughout the city.

Acadian Festival, Claire: Early July brings many ethnic festivals to Nova Scotia. This one features Acadian fiddle music, dancing, crafts, and traditional meals.

Festival of the Tartans, New Glasgow: This Scottish event in mid-July features highland piping, drumming, and a variety of traditional activities.

Chapel Island Indian Mission, Chapel Island: At the end of July, the Micmac welcome visitors to a week-long celebration of their Native culture, featuring dances, feasts, and arts and crafts.

Rockhound Round-Up, Parrsboro: Each August, amateur mineralogists and rock collectors from all over North America gather for a large swap meet and seminar.

Oktoberfest, Lunenburg: In autumn, the province's German-Canadians celebrate their heritage with traditional food, beer, music, and costumes.

Halloween, Halifax: Over the years, Halifax's celebration of Halloween has turned into a huge, spectacular street party, with costumes and music similar to those of New Orleans's Mardi Gras.

Boats at Lunenburg

Chronology

1497	John Cabot claims Nova Scotia for Britain.
1605	French explorers Samuel de Champlain and Pierre du Guast found a settlement at Port Royal.
17th century	French Settlers emigrate to Acadia; meanwhile, France and Britain quarrel over ownership of the territory.
1713	France gives the mainland peninsula to Britain under the Treaty of Utrecht but keeps Cape Breton Island.
1749	The British establish a fort and settlement at Halifax.
1755	The Acadians are forcibly deported by the British.
1758	France gives Cape Breton Island to Britain; Nova Scotia's first parliament meets in Halifax.
1763	French rule in Canada ends.
1848	Nova Scotia becomes the first British colony to be granted self-government.
1867	Nova Scotia joins the Dominion of Canada as one of four founding provinces.
1917	A French munitions ship explodes in Halifax Harbor, killing 2,000 people and destroying half the city.
1939–45	During World War II, Nova Scotia becomes the chief port for transport of troops and war supplies across the North Atlantic; an economic boom follows.
1960s and 1970s	The province's economy slumps; unemployment increases.
late 1980s	Nova Scotia begins to revive its coal mining industry and to plan the development of offshore oil and gas resources.

Further Reading

Bishop, Morris. *Champlain: The Life of Fortitude*. New York: Hippocrene, 1979.

Boudreau, Amy. *Story of the Acadians*. Gretna, LA: Pelican, 1971.

Fingard, Judith. *Jack in Port: Sailortowns of Eastern Canada*. Toronto: University of Toronto Press, 1982.

Frideres, James. *Canada's Indians: Contemporary Conflicts*. Englewood Cliffs, NJ: Prentice-Hall, 1974.

Haliburton, Thomas C. *The Clockmaker*. Reprint of 1838 edition. New York: Irvington, 1979.

Henry, Frances. *Forgotten Canadians: The Blacks of Nova Scotia*. Don Mills, Ontario: Longman, 1973.

Hocking, Anthony. *Nova Scotia*. New York: McGraw-Hill Ryerson, 1978.

Holbrook, Sabra. *Canada's Kids*. New York: Atheneum, 1983.

Law, Kevin. *Canada*. New York: Chelsea House, 1989.

Macleod, Alistair. *The Lost Salt Gift of Blood: New & Selected Stories*. Toronto: Ontario Review Press, 1988.

McNaught, Kenneth. *The Penguin History of Canada*. New York: Penguin Books, 1988.

O'Connor, D'Arcy. *The Money Pit: The Story of Oak Island and the World's Greatest Treasure Hunt*. New York: Coward, McCann & Geoghegan, 1979.

Slafter, Edmund F., ed. *Sir William Alexander and American Colonization*. New York: Franklin, Burt, 1966.

Wallis, Wilson Dallam. *The Micmac Indians of Eastern Canada*. Minneapolis: University of Minnesota Press, 1955.

Woodcock, George. *The Canadians*. Cambridge: Harvard University Press, 1980.

Index

The Bettmann Archive: pp. 16, 29, 20, 24; Diana Blume: p. 6; Clark Photographic Limited: p. 30; © Wally Hayes: pp. 5, 8, 11, 12, 14, 22, 42, 47, 49, 53, 54; Industry, Science and Technology Canada: cover, pp. 3, 9, 40, 41, 48, 51, 57, 59; National Archives of Canada: p. 23; Notman Photographic Archives, McCord Museum of Canadian History: pp. 17, 28; Nova Scotia Department of Tourism: pp. 44, 45, 55, 58; Nova Scotia Information Service: pp. 32, 33, 35, 36, 38, 39; Public Archives of Nova Scotia: pp. 22, 27, 29; Debora Smith: p. 7.

Suzanne LeVert has contributed several volumes to Chelsea House's LET'S DISCOVER CANADA series. She is the author of four previous books for young readers. One of these, *The Sakharov File*, a biography of noted Russian physicist Andrei Sakharov, was selected as a Notable Book by the National Council for the Social Studies. Her other books include *AIDS: In Search of a Killer, The Doubleday Book of Famous Americans*, and *New York*. Ms. LeVert also has extensive experience as an editor, first in children's books at Simon & Schuster, then as associate editor at *Trialogue*, the magazine of the Trilateral Commission, and as senior editor at Save the Children, the international relief and development organization. She lives in Cambridge, Massachusetts.

George Sheppard, General Editor, is a lecturer on Canadian and American history at McMaster University in Hamilton, Ontario. Dr. Sheppard holds an honors B.A. and an M.A. in history from Laurentian University and earned his Ph.D. in Canadian history at McMaster. He has taught Canadian history at Nipissing University in North Bay. His research specialty is the War of 1812, and he has published articles in *Histoire sociale/Social History, Papers of the Bibliographical Society of Canada*, and *Ontario History*. Dr. Sheppard is a native of Timmins, Ontario.

Pierre Berton, Senior Consulting Editor, is the author of 34 books, including *The Mysterious North, Klondike, Great Canadians, The Last Spike, The Great Railway Illustrated, Hollywood's Canada, My Country: The Remarkable Past, The Wild Frontier, The Invasion of Canada, Why We Act Like Canadians, The Klondike Quest*, and *The Arctic Grail*. He has won three Governor General's Awards for creative nonfiction, two National Newspaper Awards, and two ACTRA "Nellies" for broadcasting. He is a Companion of the Order of Canada, a member of the Canadian News Hall of Fame, and holds 12 honorary degrees. Raised in the Yukon, Mr. Berton began his newspaper career in Vancouver. He then became managing editor of *McLean's*, Canada's largest magazine, and subsequently worked for the Canadian Broadcasting Network and the *Toronto Star*. He lives in Kleinburg, Ontario.